King
Cecil
the Sea Horse

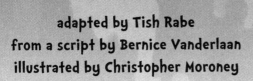

adapted by Tish Rabe
from a script by Bernice Vanderlaan
illustrated by Christopher Moroney

 A GOLDEN BOOK • NEW YORK

Based in part on *The Cat in the Hat Knows a Lot About That!* TV series (Episode 31) © CITH Productions, Inc. (a subsidiary of Portfolio Entertainment, Inc.), and Red Hat Animation, Ltd. (a subsidiary of Collingwood O'Hare Productions, Ltd.), 2010–2011.

THE CAT IN THE HAT KNOWS A LOT ABOUT THAT! logo and word mark TM 2010 Dr. Seuss Enterprises, L.P., Portfolio Entertainment, Inc., and Collingwood O'Hare Productions, Ltd. All rights reserved. The PBS KIDS logo is a registered trademark of PBS. Both are used with permission. All rights reserved.

Broadcast in Canada by Treehouse™. Treehouse™ is a trademark of the Corus® Entertainment Inc. group of companies. All rights reserved.

Seussville.com   pbskids.org/catinthehat   treehousetv.com

ISBN: 978-0-449-81010-1
Library of Congress Control Number: 2012935481
Printed in the United States of America   10 9 8 7 6 5 4 3 2
Random House Children's Books supports the First Amendment and celebrates the right to read.

"Hail, Queen Sally and Princess Panda!" said Nick. "See the horse I've made from two towels and a stick."

"King Nick," Sally said,
"I have dragons to fight.
Can you babysit for
Princess Panda tonight?"

"Babysit!" said the Cat.
"Oh, that's such fun to do.
I'm a great babysitter
and you can be, too.

"We'll go to see someone
you won't soon forget.
He's the best babysitter
that I've ever met."

"He is Cecil the Sea Horse,
and soon we will be
on a royal adventure
deep under the sea.

"Press the Shrinkamadoodle
and we'll get so small,
we'll swim with sea horses
in no time at all."

"I'm King Cecil," the king said,
"and this is my queen."
Said Nick, "You're the first
sea horse king that I've seen."

"Sea horses," the Cat said,
"you'll find out today,
give birth to their babies
in their own special way."

"When it's time to have babies,
a sea horse dad knows
he will carry the babies
wherever he goes.

"The mom puts her eggs
in a pouch on the dad."
"I carry them," said the king,
"and it isn't too bad."

"Next, I must find
a home in the sea—
a safe place to bring up
my big family.

"We need to hurry
and leave right away.
My babies are due
to be born any day!"

The king did not like
the first place that he found.
The water was rough
and it pushed them around.

"Not here," the king said,
"I am sorry to say.
If my babies stayed here,
they would be swept away."

The next place they tried
was a thick sea grass bed.
"This spot is just right
for us all," the king said.

"Something's moving," said Nick.
"I wonder, what's that?"
"The babies are hatching
right now!" said the Cat.

In seconds, the babies
started to pop
out of the king's pouch—
and they did not stop!

"Baby sea horses are really cute!" Sally said. "And each has little bumps like a crown on its head!"

Back home, Sally said,
"I love Princess Panda, I do,
but I miss the new babies."
Nick said, "Me too!"

"Surprise!" said the Cat.
"I bet you can't guess.
It's a card from King Cecil,
sent Sea Horse Express!"

"His babies are doing great.
Oh my! Joy of joys!
All two hundred and forty-eight girls
and two hundred and fifty-two boys!"

Born: June 29
Time: 3 p.m.
Place: Sea Grass Cove

Proud Parents:
King Cecil and Queen Cerise

248 Girls and 252 Boys